LITTLE
WISDOM

Member of the
Evangelical Christian
Publishers Association

Printed in the United States of America.

LITTLE WAGS OF WISDOM

BARBOUR
PUBLISHING

A HOUSE IS NOT A HOME WITHOUT A DOG.

UNKNOWN

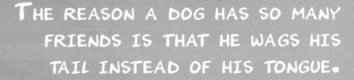

THE REASON A DOG HAS SO MANY
FRIENDS IS THAT HE WAGS HIS
TAIL INSTEAD OF HIS TONGUE.

UNKNOWN

Lessons learned as a puppy aren't
forgotten when a dog matures. If a pup witnesses
and misunderstands a playful rap from his owner,
that "rapper" could earn an enemy for life.
We can learn with maturity. Guard against
any misunderstanding that can
mushroom into an unforgiving grudge.

Dogs fetch newspapers. Dogs retrieve overthrown Frisbees. Some dogs have been known to round up sheep or help out on the ranch. Some dogs make fine babysitters when Mom or Dad leaves the room for a minute. Enjoy life's little conveniences— compliments of your dog.

DOGS KNOW THERE'S NOTHING LIKE A GOOD WALK. THEY SOMETIMES WALK WITH THEIR OWNERS, BELIEVE IT OR NOT, ON THEIR TWO BACK FEET, ONE FRONT PAW IN THE HAND OF THEIR OWNER.

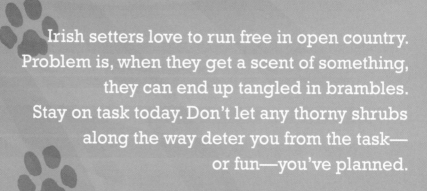

Irish setters love to run free in open country. Problem is, when they get a scent of something, they can end up tangled in brambles. Stay on task today. Don't let any thorny shrubs along the way deter you from the task— or fun—you've planned.

Dogs that go from home to home may develop aggressive, unpredictable temperaments. With lots of TLC, however, even the biggest meanies can shed the baggage of the past. They can go on to become fun-loving and loveable.

Big dogs, like Labs, enjoy sinking their teeth into hard rawhide bones. For hours they'll keep at it, simultaneously toughening and cleaning their pearly whites. Instead of nibbling at an occasional scripture, we need to tackle meaty Bible passages. Mulling over scripture builds strong convictions.

EVERY BOY WHO HAS A DOG
SHOULD ALSO HAVE A MOTHER,
SO THE DOG CAN BE FED REGULARLY.

UNKNOWN

Police dogs are often commended for their bravery. Frequently their loyalty while on duty costs them their lives. Their human officers know they are good partners and good friends. Friends like that are friends to hold onto for life. That's the kind of friend to be in return.

Some dogs sleep in their owners' beds.
Others get between-meal snacks under the table.
Such practices were never learned in obedience school.
Much of what we do in life is not taught,
but caught. Make note of the lessons
your loved ones "catch" from you.

DOGS HAVE OWNERS; CATS HAVE STAFF.
IF YOU WANT TO BE A BOSS, GET A DOG.

UNKNOWN

Cocker spaniels live for protectiveness and loyalty.
Loved ones depend on us to take care of them.
Our employers depend on us to be loyal employees.
The time is always right to play the cocker spaniel.

Assistance dogs act as ears, eyes, or stabilizers for their people. They do their duty without complaining. If we're called upon to be someone's ears or eyes, do we do it without grumbling? If an elderly family member needs help to get around, do we offer a reassuring arm?

As children, we all had a favorite cartoon dog. Whatever attracted us in our innocence to that dog may be a good trait to copy. Unless that favorite trait was scratching his ear with his hind foot.

Well-behaved dogs take their punishment to heart,
hang their heads, and don't repeat the offense.
When we want to say, "I'm sorry" and we mean it,
we shouldn't repeat the offense either.

I HAVE ALWAYS THOUGHT OF A DOG LOVER AS A
DOG THAT WAS IN LOVE WITH ANOTHER DOG.

JAMES THURBER

A DOG THAT NEVER STOPS BARKING
IS A REAL IRRITANT. 'NUFF SAID.

Mother dogs: nurturing, attentive, quiet.
Wild dogs: undependable, aggressive, loud.
When we're with our friends,
which group of canines are we most like?

English author and veterinarian James Herriot found out early in his career that small-animal care would top large-animal medicine as a money maker for animal doctors. Don't think for a minute that dogs aren't high maintenance. Just ask your local vet.

EVERY DOG HAS HIS DAY.
SO DOES EVERY PERSON.

"I TELL YOU, NOW IS THE TIME OF GOD'S
FAVOR, NOW IS THE DAY OF SALVATION."

2 CORINTHIANS 6:2 NIV

We tolerate a lot with our puppies. They whine. They get worms. They demand a lot of attention. We need to show the same patience with our whiney, sick, or demanding family members.

Baths are a nightmare for most dogs. Once in a while, however, one comes along that can't get enough of the water. It just goes to show you: There's enough diversity and spontaneity around us to keep life interesting. We just have to take—or make—the time to look.

My collie, myself: created for
the wilds, bred for home.

CHUCK MILLER

CHOCOLATE IS NOT GOOD FOR DOGS.
MAKES YOU GLAD TO BE HUMAN.

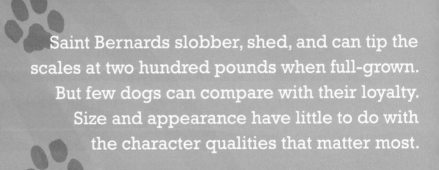

Saint Bernards slobber, shed, and can tip the scales at two hundred pounds when full-grown. But few dogs can compare with their loyalty. Size and appearance have little to do with the character qualities that matter most.

You learn in [the financial] business:
If you want a friend, get a dog.

CARL ICAHN

Hollywood costume-designer Edith Head
once said she'd never met one unspoiled star—
except for Lassie. Few of us handle stardom
or fame with Lassie-like humility.

YESTERDAY I WAS A DOG.
TODAY I'M A DOG. TOMORROW I'LL
PROBABLY STILL BE A DOG. SIGH!
THERE'S SO LITTLE ROOM FOR ADVANCEMENT.

SNOOPY

LITTLE THINGS MATTER TO GOD.
HOW WE DO OUR JOBS. HOW WE MANAGE
OUR MONEY. HOW WE TREAT OUR DOGS.

Labrador retrievers seldom meet anyone they wouldn't call "friend." They're four-legged proof that to make a friend, we must be one first.

Police dogs aren't trained to be vicious.
Play comes naturally to them. Their trainers teach them
to play to win: to search out or hold onto the prize
(illicit drugs, a criminal suspect). No matter what.
We too need to persevere—to hold
onto what's good. No matter what.

Firehouse Dalmatians, like Clydesdale-drawn water wagons, have gone the way of the dinosaur. When forced out of our job by change or downsizing, it's time to get creative. Show business might be a stretch for some of us, but if dogs and horses can do it, why not us?

Bull terriers can be tenacious.
They hold on. Unfortunately, their more common
name—"pit bulls"—has given them a stigma
that's hard to shake. Be careful when ascribing
labels to pets—or people.

Only One Woof, written by James Herriot, tells the true story of a dog who, as far as anyone knows, only barked once in his life. He barked the day he was reunited with one of his brothers—not before, or since.

Rin Tin Tin may have been television's first
famous dog. "Rinty" did some awesome stunts,
but he didn't have the staying power of Lassie.
People don't remember heroics for long.
But kindness and gentleness linger
in our memory like a fragrance.

WE SHOULD SHED ENCOURAGEMENT
JUST LIKE COLLIES SHED HAIR: EVERYWHERE,
ALL THE TIME, IN GREAT GOBS THAT CLING
TO EVERYONE WE COME IN CONTACT WITH.

CHUCK MILLER

Slow moving, obedient, and patient. That's how one website describes Saint Bernards. Sounds like a good dog to have around. It sounds so good that it makes one wonder why we don't emulate them. Except for the drooling.

Dogs have dog breath. They can't help it.
We can present a sweet fragrance
or a stench with our attitudes.
And we *can* help it.

Our lives are a Christ-like fragrance rising up to God.
But this fragrance is perceived differently by those
who are being saved and by those who are perishing.

2 CORINTHIANS 2:15 NLT

"She's a dog," compliments neither women nor aircraft. Some husbands find themselves "in the doghouse" on a forgotten anniversary. Dogs get a lot of negative press for things over which they have no control. Sometimes we do, too. Dogs just move on. So should we.

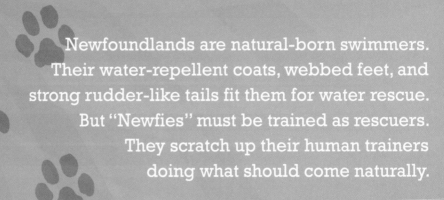

Newfoundlands are natural-born swimmers. Their water-repellent coats, webbed feet, and strong rudder-like tails fit them for water rescue. But "Newfies" must be trained as rescuers. They scratch up their human trainers doing what should come naturally.

Seldom, if ever, are there run-of-the-mill mutts at
a dog show. Dog shows are for show dogs.
Most of us aren't much good for show either.
But, like most mutts, we can have full lives that brim
with comfortable familiarity right where we live.

Hospice dogs provide undemanding companionship to people in their final days. Some patients want to pet them. Some patients are content just knowing they're close by. Knowing we're nearby—close at hand—may be all a dying friend or relative wants from us.

DOGS AREN'T BIG ON MEDICINE.
THEY'D RATHER RIFLE THROUGH A BAG OF
GARBAGE THAN TAKE ONE DEWORMING PILL.
MANY OF US FIND THE HUMBLING, NECESARY
LESSONS IN LIFE HARD PILLS TO SWALLOW, TOO.

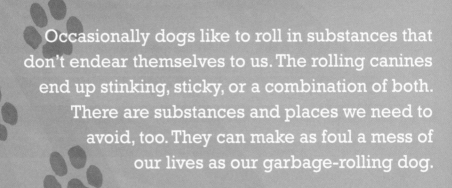

Occasionally dogs like to roll in substances that don't endear themselves to us. The rolling canines end up stinking, sticky, or a combination of both. There are substances and places we need to avoid, too. They can make as foul a mess of our lives as our garbage-rolling dog.

It's not the size of the dog in a fight,
it's the size of the fight in the dog.

MARK TWAIN

The same can be said of people.
The tricky part is in knowing
what's worth the fight.

Before you beat a dog, find out who its master is.

CHINESE PROVERB

How much better not to beat a dog,
no matter who its master is.

DOGS COME WHEN THEY'RE CALLED;
CATS TAKE A MESSAGE AND GET
BACK TO YOU LATER.

MARY BLY

SOME SAY IT'S A DOG—EAT—DOG WORLD.
THEY MUST BE CAT OWNERS.

If you want the best seat in your home,
move the dog.

UNKNOWN

We've all known dogs whose barks were worse than their bites. We tend to forget our human "barking" can be more lethal to someone than any dog bite.

A DOG THAT INTENDS TO BITE DOES NOT BARE ITS TEETH.

TURKISH PROVERB

Hunting dogs play many roles. They know how to make themselves useful. They make good companions. Even if we don't hunt, we, too, can be good companions and make ourselves useful to others.

When a dog eagerly wags his tail, all his attention is focused on the person in his line of vision. Has God enjoyed such focused attention from us today?

Picture puppies and children together.
Don't you feel better already?

SIN IS LIKE DOG POO; WHEN YOU GET SOME ON YOUR SHOE, A LITTLE IS AS BAD AS A LOT.

CHUCK MILLER

WHETHER DOBERMAN OR POODLE,
PUPPIES ARE SUCH A NICE WAY
TO START DOGS.

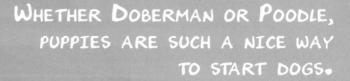

If a dog jumps in your lap, it is because he is fond of you; but if a cat does the same thing, it is because your lap is warmer.

ALFRED NORTH WHITEHEAD

Women and cats will do as they please, and men
and dogs should relax and get used to the idea.

ROBERT A. HEINLEIN

**TO LIVE LONG, EAT LIKE A CAT,
DRINK LIKE A DOG.**

GERMAN PROVERB

DOGS ARE BETTER THAN HUMAN BEINGS BECAUSE THEY KNOW BUT DO NOT TELL.

EMILY DICKINSON

There's a world of difference between the age-old expressions, "puttin' on the dog," and "goin' to the dogs." When we choose to go to an entertainment event, which of these describes what it is we're about to do?

"It is not right to take children's bread and toss it to their dogs," Jesus told a foreigner seeking His help. She responded, "Even the dogs eat the crumbs that fall from their masters' table." She got her request. (See Matthew 15:26–28 NIV). Then, as now, Jesus doesn't give us table scraps.

You can say any foolish thing to a dog, and the dog will give you this look that says, ". . .you're right! I never would've thought that!"

Dave Berry

FEW SIGHTS ARE AS PLEASING TO
THE EYE AS A BOY AND HIS DOG.

When two aircraft do battle aloft, it's called a dog fight.
When two women fight, it's called a cat fight.
Even the origins of simple things in life can't
always be understood or explained.

I used to look at (my dog)...and think, "If you were a little smarter, you could tell me what you were thinking," and he'd look at me like he was saying, "If you were a little smarter, I wouldn't have to."

FRED JUNGCLAUS

SEARCH—AND—RESCUE DOGS ARE
A NOBLE BREED. DOG CAN BE
MAN'S BEST FRIEND EVEN IN
LIFE—AND—DEATH SITUATIONS.

SLED DOGS GIVE US GOOD LESSONS
IN BOTH THE PRACTICE AND
THE VALUE OF TEAMWORK.

Few can resist a puppy.
If you're struggling to make new friends after a long-
distance move, you might try getting a pup. If still
no one ventures to make your acquaintance,
you've got at least one new friend.

The American Kennel Club was founded in 1884.
The Miss America Pageant began in 1921. Most dogs
won't make it to the AKC's top-dog categories.
Most women won't ever be Miss Congeniality, let alone
Miss America. But the best and kindest among us all
will have the longer-lasting legacies.

Scratch a dog and you'll find a permanent job.

FRANKLIN P. JONES

Encourage people. You'll have a second—
and rewarding—permanent job.

"RELATIVES ARE THE WORST FRIENDS," SAID THE FOX AS THE DOGS TOOK AFTER HIM.

DANISH PROVERB

Some dogs, like some children, know innately what they're "cut out" for. Pointers display pointing/hunting instincts as young puppies. Children as young as five or six sometimes announce, "I'm going to be a teacher (or a pilot) when I grow up!"
Our part?
Encouragement!

Afghan hounds have been described as dogs that tend to think for themselves. Sometimes they don't do well when it comes to following commands, yet they *can* be taught obedience.
Sound like anyone you know?

**THE MOST AFFECTIONATE CREATURE
IN THE WHOLE WORLD IS A WET DOG.**

AMBROSE BIERCE

IF YOU TURN THE IMAGINATION LOOSE LIKE A HUNTING DOG, IT WILL OFTEN RETURN WITH THE BIRD IN ITS MOUTH.

WILLIAM MAXWELL

Let God's Word and God's love be the herd dogs
chasing your thoughts into the prayer corral.

CHUCK MILLER

Bloodhounds are renowned for sniffing out their quarry with unmatched determination. They're neither easily nor quickly deterred from the intensity of their hunt. Sometimes we must mimic that same determination to get a job done.

A HEALTHY DOG IS MORE LIKELY
TO BE BETTER BEHAVED AND HAPPY.
SO ARE HEALTHY PEOPLE.

BEWARE OF SILENT DOGS
AND STILL WATERS.

PORTUGUESE PROVERB

[The Greyhound] is swift as a ray of light, graceful
as a swallow, and wise as a Solomon.

THE COMPLETE DOG BOOK, 1979

Exaggeration has a place in storytelling,
but that's about it.

History credits Helen Keller with bringing the first Akita to the USA. Although Akitas are loyal, devoted family pets, they have a blind spot: other dogs. Some of us have blind spots, too. Heeding God, or the counsel of a wise friend, may restore our impaired vision.

Alaskan Malamutes model hard work and endurance. In spite of their brute strength, they retain a gentle demeanor around children. Sounds like the backbone of our country: hard-working, loving fathers.

No child has a problem with Clifford, the big dog, being red. If we teach our children well, they won't be troubled by or perplexed with people whose skin color differs from theirs.

Wolfhound puppies can demolish a room an hour.
When full-grown, Wolfhounds gallop as easily as horses.
Young or full-grown, Wolfhounds need space.
Feel like you need some space today? Call the dog,
grab the leash, and get outdoors.

THE BOXER BREED TENDS TO BEGIN A FIGHT WITH THEIR FRONT PAWS, JUST LIKE A HUMAN BOXER WITH HIS GLOVED HANDS. LIKE HUMAN BOXERS, HOWEVER, FIGHTING IS NOT WHAT MAKES BOXERS DEAR TO THOSE CLOSEST TO THEM.

The 1960's cartoon character, Deputy Dawg, had two friends. But Muskie the Muskrat and Vincent Van Gopher gave him more trouble than friendship. We need to choose our friends more carefully than Deputy Dawg did.

ONE REASON A DOG CAN BE SUCH A
COMFORT WHEN YOU'RE FEELING BLUE IS
THAT HE DOESN'T TRY TO FIND OUT WHY.

UNKNOWN

In World War I, Belgian sheepdogs were trained as messengers between divisions of soldiers. They were devoted and dependable. People like people who meet those criteria, too.

Want to lower your blood pressure?
Studies have shown that petting your dog may
do just the trick. The dog will enjoy it, too.

**LIFE IS LIKE A DOGSLED TEAM.
IF YOU AIN'T THE LEAD DOG,
THE SCENERY NEVER CHANGES.**

LEWIS GRIZZARD

OLD ENGLISH SHEEPDOGS WERE,
AT ONE TIME, EXEMPT FROM TAXES
IN ENGLAND. DON'T YOU WISH
YOU KNEW THEIR SECRET?

Robertson Davies noted, "A dog is a yes-animal, very popular with people who can't afford to keep a yes-man." If you've heard nothing but "no" today from your children, your boss, or your lending institution, take some time to talk to your dog.

Rottweilers are known for their intelligence
and uncompromising guarding instinct.
Happily, many children see those
same qualities in their moms.

ANYBODY WHO DOESN'T KNOW WHAT SOAP
TASTES LIKE NEVER WASHED A DOG.

FRANKLIN P. JONES

As early as the eighteenth century, Saint Bernards rescued people from the Alpine snows. They licked the faces of unconscious victims to revive them.

Siberian Huskies transported life-saving medication during a diphtheria epidemic in Nome, Alaska, in 1925. They were used for the Byrd Antarctic Expeditions. In World War II, they were used in search and rescue. Who says dogs aren't a noble breed of animal?

The Samoyed breed carries in its face and heart
the spirit of Christmas the whole year through.

Unknown

PROPERLY TRAINED,
A MAN CAN BE A DOG'S BEST FRIEND.

COREY FORD

LHASA APSO DOGS ARE PROOF THAT
ANYONE NAMING THEM BY BREED CAN LEARN
TO SPEAK ANY LANGUAGE IN THE WORLD.

Prior to 1800 in England, bulldogs were vicious fighters. With careful breeding, these aggressors became fine pets. Likewise, "since you have heard about Jesus and learned the truth that comes from him, throw off your old sinful nature and. . .put on your new nature, created to be like God—truly righteous and holy"(Ephesians 4:21–22, 24 NLT).

If you think dogs can't count, try putting
three dog biscuits in your pocket and then
giving Fido only two of them.

PHIL PASTORET

THERE IS NO PSYCHIATRIST IN THE
WORLD LIKE A PUPPY LICKING YOUR FACE.

BERNARD WILLIAMS

TO KEEP A TRUE PERSPECTIVE OF ONE'S IMPORTANCE, EVERYONE SHOULD HAVE A DOG THAT WILL WORSHIP HIM AND A CAT THAT WILL IGNORE HIM.

DEREKE BRUCE

By and large, people who enjoy teaching animals
to roll over will find themselves happier with a dog.

Barbara Holland

There are house dogs, herding dogs, and police dogs. Like people, they all have their differing strengths and weaknesses. Why would we expect every person to be like us?

IF YOU GET TO THINKING YOU'RE A PERSON OF SOME INFLUENCE, TRY ORDERING SOMEBODY ELSE'S DOG AROUND.

WILL ROGERS

"DIGNIFIED ALOOFNESS" HAS BEEN USED TO DESCRIBE AIREDALE TERRIERS. ALOOFNESS IS A QUALITY WE NEED TO AVOID. IT SHUTS OUT PEOPLE WHO YEARN FOR INCLUSION.

Chihuahuas, clannish dogs by nature, often find themselves the only dog in a household. People who were social throughout their lives sometimes find themselves painfully alone as old age or ill health cloisters them. Maybe it's time to visit someone you know like that today. Take the dog along!

A missionary home from his time overseas was the houseguest of a couple in the church where he was ministering. As they sat around the supper table, his hostess noticed her dog looking up at their guest adoringly. "Isn't that sweet?" she cooed.
"He knows you have his bowl."

PAPILLONS THRIVE IN HOT CLIMATES AND ITALIAN GREYHOUNDS ENJOY BRISK TEMPERATURES. IT'S REASSURING TO KNOW THAT WHATEVER KIND OF CLIMATE WE LIVE IN, THERE'S A DOG OUT THERE THAT WOULD LIKE LIVING IN IT WITH US.

Centuries ago, common practice among Japanese
royalty included giving dogs as gifts.
Today the better part of wisdom says investigate
before giving a dog—especially a pricey,
rare breed of canine—to anyone.

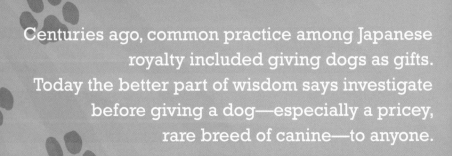

Our fiercely protective dogs may suffer short-term memory loss. If we have overnight guests, we should be the first one up the next day. Otherwise we may find our guests on one side of a chair with our snarling dog on the other.

When their keyless owner is on the outside,
dogs have been known to lock car doors from the inside.
Unfortunately, those same dogs can't unlock the doors.
With no help from our dogs, we can easily get ourselves
into bad situations from which escape is not so easy.

SOME DOGS ARE SO HIGH-STRUNG
THEY NEED MEDICATION WHEN YOUNG
CHILDREN COME TO VISIT. IF YOU'RE
A GRANDMOTHER, YOU PROBABLY KNOW
JUST HOW THOSE DOGS FEEL.

WHEN CHILDREN GROW UP WITH A PUPPY,
THEY LEARN EARLY ON HOW VALUABLE
A LIFELONG FRIENDSHIP CAN BE.

When you try a new dog food for your pet,
try something new in your own diet. Take a walk on the
culinary wild side with your pooch. You both
might find something new you like.

Prince William of Orange, history says, was saved from military attack by his dog's barked warning. Many people recount amazing stories of their dogs saving them from danger. Dogs bless us in more ways than we can count.

IF A DOG WILL NOT COME TO YOU AFTER
HAVING LOOKED YOU IN THE FACE, YOU SHOULD
GO HOME AND EXAMINE YOUR CONSCIENCE.

WOODROW WILSON

PUPPIES, LIKE CHILDREN, ARE LABOR-INTENSIVE. SO IS HOME REMODELING. THE DIFFERENCE? CHILDREN AND PUPPIES BRING JOY AND DELIGHT AT MANY POINTS ALONG THEIR "CONSTRUCTION."

Pug dogs have been described as *multum in parvo*,
which means "a lot of dog in a small space."
Most of us have met some children who are
"a lot of child in a small space."

Pekingese dogs look like flowing waves of soft fur.
Yet they are known for their stubbornness and stamina.
Some sweet-faced children have iron wills.
On dogs or people, looks can be deceiving.

A DOG CAN EXPRESS MORE WITH HIS TAIL IN SECONDS THAN HIS OWNER CAN EXPRESS WITH HIS TONGUE IN HOURS.

UNKNOWN

WHEN WORDS ARE MANY, SIN IS NOT ABSENT,
BUT HE WHO HOLDS HIS TONGUE IS WISE.

PROVERBS 10:19 NIV

Dog lovers think dogs are the best pets because they're intelligent, friendly, faithful, and fun. We don't have to be dogs for people to enjoy our company for those same reasons.

Golden retrievers like outdoor action. Labradors enjoy being with people. Assistance dogs focus all their attention and devotion on one person. Just as we recognize our dogs' differences, we need to show our children the same understanding when it comes to their unique differences.

**OH THE SADDEST OF SIGHTS
IN A WORLD OF SIN
IS A LITTLE LOST PUP
WITH HIS TAIL TUCKED IN.**

ARTHUR GUITERMAN

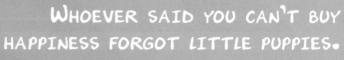

WHOEVER SAID YOU CAN'T BUY HAPPINESS FORGOT LITTLE PUPPIES.

GENE HILL

Hearing and smelling are the dog's best senses.
Sometimes we have impaired sensitivities when it
comes to others. Just like our dog warns us of a prowler
or smoldering fire, a trusted friend may alert
us of our insensitivity to someone else.

One dog expert says that if a dog is left alone too long, she'll get bored. With boredom come messes, chewed furniture, and/or incessant barking. Bored people tend to hurt more on the inside. Include someone who's bored in your plans today.

There are pedigree (purebred) dogs and mongrels (mixed-breed dogs). Too often we classify people the way we classify dogs. Only with people, those labels hurt.

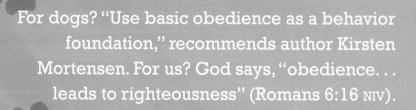

For dogs? "Use basic obedience as a behavior foundation," recommends author Kirsten Mortensen. For us? God says, "obedience. . . leads to righteousness" (Romans 6:16 NIV).

Being bred to round up sheep, Border collies are almost impossible to tire out. Most moms would say the same thing of their young children: They're impossible to tire out. If you can, give a mom of young children a short break. If you can't, pray for her.

Their names, varied as those of our dogs today, were Trusty, Speedy, and the Cook-pot. They were pets, hunters, guards. Their names are carved on stone in ancient Egyptian tombs. Dogs have a long history with people. That alone says a lot about them.

The dog of your boyhood teaches you a great deal about friendship, and love, and death; Old Skip was my brother. They had buried him under an elm tree... yet...he really lay buried in my heart.

WILLIE MORRIS

THE DOG IS THE MOST FAITHFUL OF
ANIMALS AND WOULD BE MUCH ESTEEMED
WERE IT NOT SO COMMON.

MARTIN LUTHER

Dogs adapt. In Arab lands, sighthounds rode to hunts
on camels. Their ride on the big beasts protected their
feet from the burning sands. Today those Salukis
do the same thing. Only now they ride in Jeeps.
Do we show the same adaptability as our dogs?

After World War II, dogs weren't allowed to win medals for valor anymore. That hasn't stopped them from meritorious military service. They continue to assist our men and women in uniform all over the world. We need to serve like them: sacrificially, without thought of accolades.

DOGS CAN WIN FRIENDS AND INFLUENCE PEOPLE WITHOUT EVER READING A BOOK.

E. C. McKENZIE

A unique breed of sheepdogs, Komondors, intimidate would-be attackers by staring them down. They don't need to bark or bite. Mothers learned that stare maneuver centuries ago with their children. It still works quite well—especially in church.

Marilyn Singer wrote that one of the longest scent-trails ever recorded covered over 135 miles through Kansas. The dogs kept their master on the trail until they found the horse thief. Can we show that same kind of persistence in pursuit of what's most valuable to us?

Our dogs readily learn our body language. We learn a lot about them when we understand their body language. The same applies to other people. We don't need to ask questions to learn a lot about them. Really seeing others—not just looking at them— tells us a lot.

Any woman who does not thoroughly enjoy tramping across the country on a clear frosty morning with a good gun and a pair of dogs does not know how to enjoy life.

Annie Oakley

It is true that whenever a person loves a dog, he derives great power from it.

Old Seneca Chief

When you feel lousy, puppy therapy is indicated.

SARA PARETSKY

Take yourself, or a companion who's "feeling lousy,"
to visit the local pet store.

Dogs have saved children from freezing to death. Dogs have located wandering victims of Alzheimer's disease. Research physicians are learning that dogs may be able to reliably detect cancer in humans. Be patient with your neighbor's dog. He may one day save your life!

I CARE NOT MUCH FOR A MAN'S RELIGION WHOSE DOG AND CAT ARE NOT THE BETTER FOR IT.

ABRAHAM LINCOLN

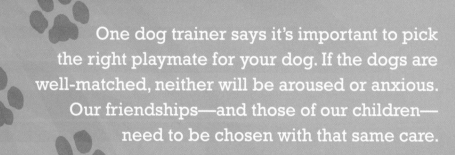

One dog trainer says it's important to pick the right playmate for your dog. If the dogs are well-matched, neither will be aroused or anxious. Our friendships—and those of our children—need to be chosen with that same care.

Anyone who sets himself up as "religious" by talking a good game is self-deceived. This kind of religion is hot air. . . . Real religion. . .is this: Reach out to the homeless and loveless in their plight, and guard against corruption from the godless world.

JAMES 1:26–27 MSG

Want to teach your children a fun song to sing? Bob Merrill's 1950s classic, "How Much Is That Doggie in the Window," might be just the thing to brighten a sunless day.

My dog does have his failings. . .but unlike me, he's not afraid of what other people think of him or anxious about his public image.

Gary Kowalski

THORNS MAY HURT YOU, MEN DESERT YOU,
SUNLIGHT TURN TO FOG; **B**UT YOU'RE NEVER
FRIENDLESS EVER, IF YOU HAVE A DOG.

DOUGLAS MALLOCK

A young girl's recovery from a serious accident
stalled—until someone brought a dog to visit.
The seven-year-old's healing began sometime between
the dog pulling her in her wheelchair and his
offering to shake her hand before he left.
Given the opportunity, dogs make good doctors.

Some dogs are trained in search and rescue.
Others are trained as therapy dogs and provide people
with comfort. There are even dogs who multitask
in these areas. If you can multitask well,
be glad of your ability. You're blessed.

Pair a person with a canine and you have
a powerful partnership.

DONNA M. JACKSON

With God as your senior partner, you have
a far more powerful partnership.

A DOG TEACHES A BOY FIDELITY,
PERSEVERANCE, AND TO TURN AROUND
THREE TIMES BEFORE LYING DOWN.

ROBERT BENCHLEY

Dogs have a body temperature that's normally higher than ours. On those cold, lonely nights, curl up with your furry heating pad. It won't increase your heating bill one bit.

Pet specialist John C. Wright says dogs should never be given as gifts to teach a child responsibility. Rather, have the child take out the garbage or make his bed. Dogs require a big investment in time. Beware of handing off—or "biting off"— too much responsibility.

IT'S FUNNY HOW DOGS AND CATS KNOW
THE INSIDE OF FOLKS BETTER THAN
OTHER FOLKS DO, ISN'T IT?

ELEANOR H. PORTER

OUTSIDE OF A DOG, A BOOK IS MAN'S BEST FRIEND. INSIDE OF A DOG, IT'S TOO DARK TO READ.

GROUCHO MARX

Dogs know a storm is coming before we do. Seizure-alert dogs can alert their owners up to an hour before their owner suffers a seizure. Be thankful for the heads-up your dog gives you in a variety of circumstances.

It's a myth that dogs won't bite the hand that feeds them. Biting is the dog's way of saying, "Get away from my food!" Before retaliating in kind when someone "bites your head off" at work or school, give some thought to the "why" behind that verbal attack.

THE DOG WAS CREATED ESPECIALLY FOR CHILDREN. HE IS THE GOD OF FROLIC.

HENRY WARD BEECHER

NO ONE APPRECIATES THE VERY SPECIAL GENIUS OF YOUR CONVERSATION AS A DOG DOES.

CHRISTOPHER MORLEY

Just like children, dogs behave differently in identical settings. Some shepherding dogs like to play the dominant/submissive role with their charges. Other breeds like to watch and chase their sheep. If we pay attention, we can learn which type of training works best—for our kids and our dogs.

A German proverb says the silent dog is the first to bite.
Politicians learn quickly that listening ears surround
them—even when they choose to whisper.
We're all wise to watch what we say.

EVERY PUPPY SHOULD HAVE A BOY.

ERMA BOMBECK

**WOULD EVERY PUPPY AGREE
WITH THAT STATEMENT?**

Before motorized vehicles and sirens came along, Dalmatians cleared the way for the horse-drawn water wagons going to fires. Nowadays, Dalmatians find themselves little more than mascots for fire departments. But they can teach fire safety to children. Aren't you glad that "out of a job" doesn't mean "out of options"?

Believe it or not, assistance dogs are taught to disobey
in special circumstances. "Intelligent disobedience"
will keep them from permitting their blind owner
to cross a traffic-free—but torn up—street.
We practice "intelligent disobedience" before God
sometimes. But it doesn't bring God's commendation.

All dogs have webbed feet, but few go on
to become good water-rescue dogs. People, too,
have many of the same physical characteristics,
but each excels in different areas. Cheer the
unique giftedness of others and enjoy your own.

If dogs don't have a pack of dogs to hang with,
they're just as happy hanging with a bunch of people.
We say our dog is "a part of the family."
Our favorite canine would say we're "part of
his pack." Togetherness—for dogs
and people—means connection.

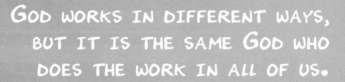

GOD WORKS IN DIFFERENT WAYS,
BUT IT IS THE SAME GOD WHO
DOES THE WORK IN ALL OF US.

1 CORINTHIANS 12:6 NLT

Someone noted that dogs aren't partial to people who are rich and famous. What's inside a person captures their heart. What captures our hearts when we look at others?

Ever found yourself or your dog "barking up the wrong tree"? With a solitary command, the dog will leave that tree without a second glance. Usually, it takes a little more for us to humble ourselves and admit our mistakes.

ONE OF THE GREATEST GIFTS A DOG CAN GIVE US IS THE GIFT OF LAUGHTER. THAT'S ONE OF THE GREATEST GIFTS ANY OF US CAN GIVE TO ANOTHER.

A PUPPY PLAYS WITH EVERY PUP HE MEETS,
BUT AN OLD DOG HAS FEW ASSOCIATES.

JOSH BILLINGS

ARE YOU A "PUPPY" OR AN "OLD DOG"?
IF YOU WANT TO FEEL YOUNGER,
A NEW FRIEND MAY BE BETTER
THAN VITAMINS.

Most of us have heard of the *Titanic*. Few of us have heard of Rigel, the Newfoundland on board that fated ship. Rigel barked at the rescue ship, *Carpathia*. Those in the lifeboat he swam in front of were saved. Even a wet dog can be a hero.

Assistance dogs can be taught—and have learned how—to do such diverse tasks as making the bed and doing the laundry. Talk about talent!

OF ALL THE THINGS **I** MISS FROM
VETERINARY PRACTICE, PUPPY BREATH IS
ONE OF THE MOST FOND MEMORIES.

D**R**. T**OM** C**AT**

THE GODLY CARE FOR THEIR ANIMALS.

PROVERBS 12:10 NLT

Maryland Task Force One Urban Search and Rescue Team member Bob Sessions searched for people with his rescue dogs after the September 11, 2001, attack on the World Trade Center and the Pentegon. He said, "There's nothing that can replace the precision of a dog's nose—and absolutely nothing that can replace a dog's heart."

When the dog days of summer sap your energy, let them remind you to refill your pooch's bowl with fresh, cool water. While you're at it, offer a cold beverage to the neighbor mowing his lawn.

No symphony orchestra ever
played music like a two-year-old
girl laughing with a puppy.

Bern Williams

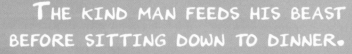

THE KIND MAN FEEDS HIS BEAST BEFORE SITTING DOWN TO DINNER.

HEBREW PROVERB

The best way to get a puppy is to beg for a little brother—and they'll settle for a puppy every time.

WINSTON PENDLETON